495

A Stepping-Stone Book

LEADERS, LAWS, AND CITIZENS

The Story of Democracy and Government

By William Wise

Illustrated by Mila Lazarevich

821

Parents' Magazine Press—New York

Library of Congress Cataloging in Publication Data
Wise, William
      Leaders, laws, and citizens.

    (A Stepping-Stone Book)
    SUMMARY: A simple history of government emphasizing
the democracy of the United States.
      1. United States—Politics and government—Juvenile
literature.   2. Democracy—Juvenile literature.
[1. United States—Politics and government.   2. Demo-
cracy]   I. Lazarevich, Mila, illus.   II. Title.
III. Title: The story of democracy and government.
[JK34.W57]   320.4'73   72-3468
ISBN 0-8193-0627-4 (lib. bdg.)

Contents

1. Rules of the Game

We can live happily with other people only if we agree to follow a number of different rules.

Sometimes we need rules in order to get things done. At school, for instance, we must have a rule that tells us when classes begin, and when they end. Without such a rule, we would not know when to go to school, or when to leave.

Sometimes we need rules just to have fun. We could not play games like baseball or hopscotch unless everyone agreed to follow a set of rules.

At home with our families, we need rules, too. Some families have a rule that everyone helps to clean up after supper. In other families, the children are expected to take care of their clothes, toys, or pets.

What are some of the special rules in your own family? Are there any you dislike, because they seem unfair? Can you ever dislike a rule that *is* fair?

What kinds of things should children have to do at home? Should they take care of their clothes? Their toys? Their pets?

Some rules, like our traffic laws, are meant to keep people from hurting one another. When drivers go too fast, they often have accidents. So our traffic laws tell a driver how fast it is safe to go.

If a driver is caught speeding, a policeman gives him a summons to appear in court. Later, a judge decides his case. The driver may have to pay a fine for breaking the law. Or the judge may take away his driver's license, or give him some other kind of punishment.

Every country needs many different laws to help its citizens. Smaller places, like states, cities, and towns, must have their own laws, too.

Good laws can serve us in many ways. They can protect us against those who try to harm us. They can help us to share things fairly with others. Often they can keep us from quarreling with strangers—or with our friends.

Laws, however, can be bad as well as good. A law is bad if it lets people take advantage of us. Or a law is bad if it robs us of our rights, property, or freedom.

And even good laws do not stay good forever. Times change. When they do, lawmakers must

write new laws. Or they must bring old laws up to date.

Years ago, when cars were new, a traffic law was written in England. It said that no car should go faster than three miles an hour. It also said that a man with a red flag had to walk ahead of the driver. His job was to warn people with horses that a noisy car was coming.

At first it was a good law. It kept horses from becoming frightened and hurting people. But then

cars replaced horses on the road. After that the law
was no longer needed. When the lawmakers realized
this, they wrote a new traffic law. It allowed cars to
go faster. And it said nothing about a man walking
on the road with a red flag.

For a long time, we have made many different
laws, and then have replaced them with newer ones.
Still our search goes on—a search for better rules, to
help us live more happily in a changing world.

2. Chiefs and Kings

Thousands of years ago people needed rules, just as we do today. Usually these early people lived in a large family called a tribe. By having certain rules the members of a tribe could work together and share their food, tools, and shelter.

In many tribes the best hunter became the chief, or leader. Often he was helped by a council of

10

wise old men. The members of a council knew all the rules of the tribe. So they could judge a quarrel fairly. Then they could tell the chief what ought to be done.

Sometimes, though, there was no time for the council to talk things over. When the tribe went hunting, there had to be one leader to give orders. And the other hunters had to obey him at once. Otherwise the animals they were hunting would escape, and no one in the tribe would get anything to eat.

After a long while, most tribes gave up hunting and became farmers. The number of people grew. In time, towns and cities were built, and the first countries were formed.

These countries were ruled by kings, who needed laws for their people. Kings also needed government officials to decide quarrels, and tax collectors to gather money and goods for the royal treasury. And kings had to have soldiers, to arrest those who broke the law.

In many countries the laws were very cruel. People caught cheating or stealing often were put to death. There also were large numbers of slaves. These helpless people could be bought and sold like any other kind of property. They had few rights under the law.

Free citizens, of course, were better off than
slaves. But they had their troubles, too. They did
not govern themselves. They could not change
unfair laws or write new ones. The king and his
officials decided everything. If a citizen did not like
what the government decided, there was little he
could do about it.

In most countries, when a king was good and
wise, the people were content. But when a king was
evil or foolish—and many kings were—then the
people lived in misery, with no way of making their
lives any better.

3. First Steps to Freedom

Long after the first kings began to rule, a new kind
of government was tried in the Greek city of
Athens. Instead of having a king, the citizens of
Athens chose their own leaders and made their own
laws. We call this kind of government a democracy.

Every citizen in Athens took part in the
government. At the age of eighteen, a man began to
go to meetings in the Assembly. Here he helped to

write new laws and decide other questions. When he grew older, he was chosen as a leader or a judge.

Athens did not have a full democracy, though. Women, slaves, and foreigners were not citizens in Athens. So they could not vote in the Assembly, serve as judges, or help to run the city.

Many of our ideas about justice and freedom were first thought of by the Greeks, and by the Romans who came after them.

But then the Roman Empire fell to its enemies. The Western World entered what we call the Dark Ages. For hundreds of years, most people had no rights at all. They lived under kings and noblemen who did as they pleased. In many places the common man was a serf—a kind of slave.

Yet, very slowly, people began to find new ways to gain justice and freedom. In Iceland and Switzerland, assemblies of common people started to meet, in order to decide political questions. Then, about eight hundred years ago, the noblemen of England met with King John, at a place called

Runnymede. The noblemen thought they didn't have as many rights as they should have, and made the king sign an agreement, which became known as the *Magna Carta.*

In the *Magna Carta,* or Great Charter, King John agreed that every free Englishman had the right to a fair trial. No citizen could be fined too heavily, either. The king also agreed to stop cheating the farmers in his kingdom. When he wanted food, King John agreed to pay the farmers a fair price.

As the years passed, the people of England gained other rights. They elected their own leaders to represent them in Parliament. These representatives helped to write new laws. They also could protest unfair acts of the nobles or the king.

By the early 1600s, an Englishman no longer was a serf, but a citizen with certain rights under the law. Often, too, he was a man who wanted to live in even greater freedom. So his eyes turned west, to a new land, called America, that lay beyond the seas.

4. In Early America

Almost four hundred years ago, the first settlers left their homes in England and sailed to North America. They brought with them a number of ideas about liberty and self-government. Soon they began to put some of those ideas to work.

In 1619, an election was held in the colony of Virginia. All men over the age of sixteen cast a ballot. Women, though, were not permitted to vote. The men of the colony elected twenty-two representatives, who met with the governor and

wrote several laws. It was the first meeting of an elected assembly in the New World.

A year later the Pilgrims arrived at Plymouth, in their ship, the *Mayflower*. From the beginning they were faced with many problems. They had to gather food for the winter. They had to build homes. They also had to come to an understanding with the Indians.

In order to get things done, the Pilgrims signed an agreement among themselves, called the Mayflower Compact. It said that the Plymouth settlement would follow certain democratic rules.

20

The Pilgrims would vote on different questions. The side with the most votes would win. Those on the losing side would accept the wishes of the majority.

Most early American settlements, like Plymouth, were very small. So it was easy for people to share in running their local government. This helped democratic ideas to grow from the start.

In New England, the center of a settlement was the village green. Around the green stood a meeting house, and the homes of the most important citizens.

From time to time, a town meeting was held in the meeting house. All the citizens of the village or town came and took part.

At a town meeting the people talked about their local problems. Sometimes they talked about building a public road, or raising money for the village school.

Sometimes people argued about a new law. Maybe it was a law that permitted cows to be turned loose in the village fields. Or a law to stop people from cutting down too many trees. After the argument, or debate, a vote would be taken. And the side with the most votes would win.

At first the early American settlements were
surrounded by Indian tribes. The Indians often were
peaceful and friendly. But not always. Sometimes a
tribe grew angry, and attacked the white people
who had taken their land.

Because of this danger, a citizen had to do his
share to protect the settlement where he lived. In a
New England village, every man over seventeen was
expected to arm himself with a musket. He also had
to keep some gunpowder handy, as well as bullets
and a supply of matches.

Several times a year each citizen went to the village green to drill with the home guard. On certain nights, he took his turn patrolling the village. While on patrol he kept a sharp eye out for Indians—and for wolves.

Boys between ten and seventeen also were expected to do their share. They were taught to

shoot a bow and arrow, a pistol, and a musket. If an
Indian attack came, they could help. When they
reached eighteen, they joined the home guard, or
militia. Sometimes girls learned to load and shoot
firearms, too, especially if they lived in a house that
stood far from the village green.

Before the American colonies were a hundred
years old, democracy already had taken root among
the settlers. By then, a number of Americans were
making their own laws, defending their homes, and
governing themselves.

5. The New Country

Great changes took place in our land about two hundred years ago. In 1775, the Revolutionary War broke out between the American colonies and Great Britain. After six years of fighting, the colonies won the war. They gained their independence, and became thirteen free and separate American states.

Before long, people in the thirteen states decided to form a new, democratic nation—the United States of America. They also decided to live under a set of laws called the Constitution, laws under which we still live today.

The Constitution of the United States was written in Philadelphia, in 1787. Since then, it has been changed, or amended, many times.

The first ten amendments were added almost at once. They are known as the Bill of Rights. Among other things, they guarantee freedom of speech and religion, and the right of every citizen to a fair trial.

After the Constitution had been written and signed, our country began to grow. Thousands of families crossed the ocean from Europe, and became American citizens. Some of them traveled west, and took up farming. Others built towns and cities. Soon, several new states were added to the original thirteen.

   As the years passed, the United States continued
to change. During the Civil War, President
Abraham Lincoln issued the Emancipation
Proclamation, putting an end to slavery in our
country. During the following months all black
Americans became free, and a great evil finally was
stopped.

From time to time, other important changes took place. For a long while, American women were not allowed to vote, or to serve in the government. To gain their political rights, they began to hold protest meetings. They called themselves "suffragettes," and marched in parades. Some of their leaders were arrested and taken to prison. Finally a new law was passed. It gave American women the same political rights as American men.

But not every change in America was for the best. About a hundred years ago, a number of states and cities began to be ruled by a new kind of political leader, called a "boss." The worst boss of all probably was William Marcy Tweed of New York.

"Boss" Tweed broke many laws. He cheated, to win elections. He stole millions of dollars from New York City. Newspapermen wrote stories about him, telling what he had done. A famous cartoonist, Thomas Nast, drew pictures of Tweed, to stir the people's anger.

In time, Boss Tweed was caught and brought to

"WHAT ARE YOU LAUGHING AT? TO THE VICTOR BELONG THE SPOILS."

trial. After being convicted, he was put in jail. But the harm had been done. The millions were gone—stolen from the people of New York by an evil and greedy leader.

Today we have many laws to keep men like Boss Tweed from running our cities and states. Mostly, these laws work fairly well. Yet bad leaders always can return, if we grow careless and let them. To keep this from happening we must take an interest in our government. And on election day everyone must be sure to go to the polls and vote. This includes young people from eighteen to twenty-one, who now, because of a Constitutional amendment, have the right to vote.

6. City, State, and Nation

Under our Federal Constitution, the United States government is divided into three parts.

The legislative branch, or Congress, writes our nation's laws.

The executive branch carries out those laws.

The judicial branch decides which laws agree with the Constitution, and which do not. Laws that do not agree are said to be "unconstitutional," and cannot be used.

The leader of the executive branch of our government is the president of the United States. He is our country's highest official, and is elected by the voters of all fifty states.

The president serves four years. During that time, he and his family live in the White House, in

Washington, D.C. Sometimes a president is elected to a second term. But after that he must leave office, for no president now may serve more than two terms.

Congress, or the legislative branch of our government, is made up of the Senate and the House of Representatives.

A hundred senators, two from each state, serve in the Senate. A senator's term is six years, and he may be re-elected any number of times by the people of his state.

Members of the House of Representatives, or congressmen, serve for two years. Each congressman is elected by the people who live in his congressional district. Congressional districts are set up according to the number of people who live in a section of a city or town. New York City has many congressmen. But some small towns share their congressman with other small towns nearby. A congressman, like a senator, may be re-elected any number of times.

At the head of the judicial branch of our government are nine judges, or justices, of the Supreme Court. A Supreme Court justice is not elected by the voters. He is nominated by the president, and approved by a majority vote of the Senate. His term on the Supreme Court is for life, unless he chooses to resign.

The United States government serves all the people in our country. Its laws are the supreme laws of our land.

But they are not the only laws that help and protect Americans. Under the Constitution, each state has the power to make certain laws for itself. Each state also is allowed to have its own government. The head of the executive branch is the state governor. He is elected by the voters of his state, and usually serves a four-year term.

Each state has its own constitution. Under it, large areas of the state, like counties and districts, are permitted to have their own governments, too.

Local communities in the state also have their own governments. So people who live in cities, towns, and villages can take a direct part in governing themselves.

In many American cities, the legislative branch of government is called the City Council. The members, or councilmen, live in the city, and are elected by other local citizens.

Most often, the executive branch is run by a mayor, or by a city manager. A mayor is elected by the voters. A city manager is appointed by the City Council. Though they may do a number of things differently, their jobs in many ways are alike. So it is hard to say if a city is better off with a city manager or with a mayor.

If your city has a mayor, you will usually find his office in a building called City Hall. Often a large

council room is in the same building. Every few
weeks the mayor and the council hold a public
meeting in the council room.

At such meetings, different city problems are
discussed. Perhaps a new school is needed. When
can it be built? And where? How much will the
land cost? And will the new school mean higher
taxes?

Then the mayor offers a plan to buy the land.
The council debates his plan. Some members are for

it, some against. Soon the meeting is thrown open to the public. This gives every citizen a chance to express his opinion, and to influence the council's decision. Finally the council votes on the plan. If it is passed it becomes an ordinance, or city law.

The mayor of a city has many responsibilities. He must carry out the ordinances passed by the City Council. He must offer a budget each year for the council's approval. The budget tells how the city's money will be spent.

A mayor is responsible for every department in the city's government. He must make sure that the public health department, the police, the fire

department, and the department of parks all provide the best possible help and service to the people of the city. And the mayor must see that the department of finance has enough money, so that city workers in every department can be paid.

It is hard work to run a city, state, or nation. For that reason we must try to elect good public officials, who will serve in both our national and local governments.

7. Election Time

One of the most important events in a democracy is the election of public officials. Sometimes in America we vote for local leaders, like our councilman or the mayor. Sometimes we vote for higher officials, like a senator or the president.

Long before election day, a number of men and women announce that they are candidates for office. Some run as "independents," without the help of a political party. But most are nominated as party candidates and run with their party's backing. In some cases, a candidate must win a primary election first. Only then does he receive his party's help and support.

A political party—like the Republican or the Democratic party—may favor a candidate for a number of different reasons. Perhaps the candidate has some good new ideas that the people will like, and the party thinks he will win many votes. Perhaps he already has served in government, and has proved that he can do a good job. Usually, some important party members talk with the candidate before they choose him. And they decide that he will carry out the political program of the party if he is elected.

Every four years in the United States we elect a president. A presidential campaign is the most important one we have, and lasts several months.

The candidates are heard on radio and television.
Their pictures and speeches are printed in the
newspapers. By election day the voters have learned
a great deal about the candidates, and what they
plan to do if they win.

As election time draws near, thousands of
Americans take part in presidential and local
campaigns. They help the candidates by mailing
letters and telephoning the voters. They also
perform many other jobs. Most of these workers do
not get paid for what they do. They are volunteers,

who think it important to elect their candidates.

Often, too, they enjoy the fun and excitement of an election campaign. All kinds of elections can be exciting. Sometimes it's fun to run a campaign at school, and to follow it with a vote. There are a number of ways to do this. One way is to run the campaign in your own classroom.

When you begin, have everyone in the class write his name on a separate piece of paper. Each piece should then be folded several times, and put into a hat, a paper bag, or a covered box.

Shake the pieces around for awhile, until they are all mixed together. Now draw out two, unfold them, and read off the names. They are the two candidates who will run in the election.

Several more names can then be drawn. They will be the candidates' helpers. They will make up the election teams, during the campaign.

Following this, the class should decide what the election will be about. Maybe there is soon to be a class trip. One candidate favors going to the zoo. The other candidate favors going to the museum.

After each side knows what it stands for, both teams can start to make some election posters.

Each team should try to think of a good campaign slogan. These can be painted on the posters. The slogans also can be written on slips of paper, which will be passed out later to the class as campaign handbills.

If there is time, a team might try to make up its own campaign song, by using a tune that somebody knows.

At the close of the campaign, each candidate gives a short speech, which he and his team have written. His speech should tell the class why it would be better to vote for him, rather than for his opponent.

Once the campaign is over, the voting begins. When your turn comes, you walk by yourself to the ballot box in the corner. You have a pencil and paper, and you write down one of the names. You fold up your ballot, and put it into the ballot box. Then you leave, so that the next person can vote.

No one knows which name you have written down. You have used a secret ballot. There are good reasons for voting in secret. Suppose both candidates were your friends. If the voting were not secret, they would know whom you had voted for. Then the one you had *not* voted for would probably feel hurt or angry.

After everyone in the class has voted, the ballot box is opened, and the ballots are taken out and counted. The candidate with the most votes wins the election. Maybe the zoo side has won. Or maybe the museum side. Either way, some of the class will be unhappy because they have not gotten what they wanted.

But the class is a democracy. The losing side must accept the wishes of the majority. And the next time, those on the losing side may turn out to be the winners.

8. We Give and We Receive

Every democratic government must have money, in order to serve the needs of its people. In America, most government money is raised through taxes. Nobody likes it, but good citizens know that taxes must be paid.

There are many different kinds of taxes in America. We pay an income tax on the money we earn. We pay a sales tax if we buy a football, a doll, or a book like the one you are reading now.

People who own a house or land pay a property, or real estate tax. A company that makes a profit pays a business tax. We pay an entertainment tax when we go to a movie or a ball game, and a transportation tax when we take a train or an airplane. If we buy a car, radio, or watch that was made in another country, we usually pay an import tax.

Some of our tax money goes to the federal government, in Washington, D.C. Some goes to our state, county, and city governments. In return for our tax money, each of these governments gives us the benefits and services that all Americans want and need.

The federal government in Washington does a great many jobs for us. Some of these jobs we could

not do for ourselves. It makes our postage stamps, our paper money, and our coins. It signs agreements with other countries. To keep us safe, it runs our armed forces—the Army, Navy, Air Force, Coast Guard, and Marine Corps. It also runs our space program, and sends our astronauts to the moon.

Our government in Washington uses the F.B.I. to arrest people who have broken federal laws. It makes rules for farmers and businessmen, and often lends money to help them. It makes other rules for running airlines, buses, and trains.

Our federal government builds roads, canals, and harbors. It builds houses in our cities, and dams on our lakes and rivers. It spends millions of dollars every year to help people who are poor, old, sick, or hungry.

Regional and local governments—state and
county, city and town—serve us in many ways, too.
They run our schools, public libraries, and hospitals.
Many times they get money from the federal
government to help them.

In addition, regional and local governments keep our roads and streets in repair. They try to stop the pollution of our air and water. Local governments provide us with a police force, to protect us from lawbreakers, and with a fire department, to protect us from fires.

Local governments also hire sanitation workers to collect our garbage, and build incinerators to dispose of it. They provide our homes with the sewer, gas, and water pipes we need. They hire inspectors to make sure that food stores and restaurants sell only clean, healthy food. They hire other inspectors to make sure that our homes, schools, and office buildings are safe.

None of these services are free. We pay for them with our taxes. But the system does seem to be fair. So, unless we can think of a better one, we probably will go on paying our taxes—and grumbling about them—for a long time to come.

9. Good Citizens

No democracy ever can be strong without good citizens. But the question often is asked: "What really makes somebody a good citizen?"

There is no simple answer. A good citizen certainly tries to obey the law. He does not take advantage of others. He treats public property, like a playground slide or a park bench, as carefully as he treats his own possessions.

Good citizens interest themselves in other people,
and try to help them. They serve as volunteers,
working with the handicapped and the blind. They
serve in hospitals, where they visit the sick and the
elderly, and try to cheer them up. They join
organizations like the Police Athletic League, and
run sports programs for children.

Many people also volunteer to serve on school, library, and election boards, planning committees, and parent-teacher associations. By taking an active interest in local problems, they help the city, town, or village where they live.

Each year, thousands of American children join the Boy Scouts, the Girl Scouts, and the Camp Fire

Girls. Through these organizations, and others like them, children, too, are able to help their local communities.

In many American towns and cities, a volunteer organization, called the League of Women Voters, has long been doing a very special job. For more than fifty years, the League has tried to strengthen our democracy, by studying political questions and then publishing the facts. The League also has tried to get more people interested in politics and government. And it has kept reminding Americans of the need to go to the polls and vote.

Yet today, millions of American men and women still fail to take part in our elections. Perhaps they do not know how long it has taken people to gain some of the rights and freedoms that we enjoy in the United States. Or perhaps they do not realize how easy it is to lose those rights and freedoms, even in a democracy like ours.

Index

Date Due

AUG. 1970			
AUG. 1978			

Code 4386-04, CLS-4, Broadman Supplies, Nashville, Tenn.,
Printed in U.S.A.